FAKE NEWS

by Kari A. Cornell

BrightPoint Press

San Diego, CA

BrightPoint Press

© 2020 BrightPoint Press
an imprint of ReferencePoint Press, Inc.
Printed in the United States

For more information, contact:
BrightPoint Press
PO Box 27779
San Diego, CA 92198
www.BrightPointPress.com

LIBRARY OF CONGRESS CATALOGING-IN-PUBLICATION DATA

Names: Cornell, Kari A., author.
Title: Fake news / by Kari A. Cornell.
Description: San Diego : ReferencePoint Press, Inc., 2020. | Includes
    bibliographical references and index.
Identifiers: LCCN 2019003313 (print) | LCCN 2019008914 (ebook) | ISBN
    9781682827161 (ebook) | ISBN 9781682827154 (hardcover)
Subjects: LCSH: Fake news--Juvenile literature.
Classification: LCC PN4784.F27 (ebook) | LCC PN4784.F27 C67 2020 (print) |
    DDC 070.4/3--dc23
LC record available at https://lccn.loc.gov/2019003313

CONTENTS

TIMELINE

1690
Benjamin Harris prints the first newspaper in the American colonies. It is called *Publick Occurrences, Both Foreign and Domestick*. Authorities in Boston, Massachusetts, shut down the paper.

1791
The First Amendment to the US Constitution is adopted. It protects a person's right to free speech and press.

1500   1600   1700   1800   1900

1790s
The *National Gazette* and *Gazette of the United States* publish fake news stories.

1926
The Society of Professional Journalists publishes the first Journalism Code of Ethics. This is a guide for journalists. It requires that illustrations, interviews, and quotes in newspapers be truthful.

2016
Donald Trump is a candidate for president of the United States. People post pro-Trump fake news to social media sites.

January–March 2018
Facebook deletes more than 500 million fake accounts to fight fake news.

2000   **2005**   **2010**   **2015**   **2020**

June 2017
Germany becomes the first country to pass a law to control fake news.

April 2018
Malaysia passes the Anti-Fake News Act. Many people oppose this act. They fear its purpose is to limit free speech. The government later overturns the act.

THE SPREAD OF FAKE NEWS

Strange stories appeared on the internet during the 2016 presidential election. They were about Hillary Clinton or Donald Trump. Trump and Clinton were running for president. The stories were pro-Trump. Some spread rumors about Clinton. Others made positive claims about Trump. One story said that Pope Francis

Donald Trump delivers a victory speech after winning the 2016 presidential election.

endorsed Trump. These stories were

false. Yet they appeared on social

media websites.

The 2016 presidential election was a very close race.

Teenagers in Macedonia posted many

of these stories. The teens searched

the internet for fake articles. They wrote

shocking headlines. They created 140 fake news sites. They reposted the articles to these sites. These sites had names that sounded like real news sources. One was called NewYorkTimesPolitics.com.

Most of the teens did not care about US politics. They were only interested in making money. Few jobs are available in Macedonia. The teens made money by reposting fake news articles. Advertisements appeared in these articles. The teens were paid every time a reader clicked on an ad. They also made money when the stories were reposted and shared.

They found that pro-Trump stories got the most shares and likes. Soon they only reposted pro-Trump stories.

CONCERNS ABOUT FAKE NEWS

Trump won the election. People began to wonder whether fake news influenced the election. These stories had not only come from Macedonia. They had also come from Russia. Bots in Russia had posted fake pro-Trump news on social media. A bot automatically follows or replies to social media posts. It also creates posts. The bots used fake Twitter accounts to share fake news. The accounts appeared to be

People protested Trump's ties to Russia at a 2019 march in San Francisco, California.

Republican voters from the Midwest. Clinton

called out these stories in a speech. She

said, "It's now clear that so-called fake

Hillary Clinton speaks to supporters at a rally in 2016.

news can have real-world consequences."[1]

These stories may have contributed to her

election loss.

  Today, people continue to have concerns

about fake news. Fake news remains

widespread. Journalists and activists

fight fake news with facts. Educators help

students recognize fake news. Their efforts

might reduce the spread of fake news in

the future.

CHAPTER ONE

WHAT IS FAKE NEWS?

The term *fake news* describes media that appears to come from real news outlets but is made up. It also refers to stories that are exaggerated. **Conspiracy theories** are one type of fake news. These are beliefs that powerful organizations are secretly causing certain events.

Some news sources use shocking and exaggerated headlines to attract readers.

Some politicians use the term incorrectly. They call news they do not like or agree with "fake news." Trump used the term often in speeches and interviews. He also used it in social media posts. The term is

A man protests Fox News at a rally in North Carolina in 2014.

often overused. Many people are confused

about its meaning. In a 2018 survey,

51 percent of Americans defined fake news

as any news politicians do not agree with.

THE BEGINNING OF FAKE NEWS

People have been publishing fake news stories for many years. Broadsides were published in the American **colonies** beginning in the 1640s. Broadsides were like posters. They were single sheets of paper with print on one side. They announced the news. They also contained songs and illustrations. They were distributed throughout a town or city.

Broadsides built support for people in power. The news reports were often biased. **Bias** is the favoring of one view over another. Reports were influenced by

John Winthrop helped found the Massachusetts Bay Colony in 1630. Winthrop and other leaders were very religious.

a writer's beliefs. These beliefs were often related to politics and religion. News stories included only one point of view.

In 1690, the first newspaper was printed in the American colonies. Benjamin Harris published it in Boston, Massachusetts.

It was called *Publick Occurrences, Both*

Foreign and Domestick. It was four pages

long. The English were **allied** with a Native

American tribe. Harris did not like this

alliance. This view came through in a story

he wrote. He also spread rumors about the

king of France. England was at war with

France. Harris's political views influenced

his writing.

Harris planned to print his newspaper

monthly. But Boston authorities

shut it down. People who wanted to

publish something needed a license.

The government of Massachusetts gave out this license. Harris did not have one. Authorities also did not like the stories he published.

THE REVOLUTIONARY WAR

In the late 1700s, some colonists wanted to overthrow British rule. They wanted to be independent. This led to the Revolutionary War (1775–1783). Some colonists wrote exaggerated stories. These stories spread rumors about the government. John and Samuel Adams were cousins. They lived in Massachusetts. They wrote anti-government stories.

Samuel Adams was a politician and one of the founding fathers of the United States.

The colonies became independent in 1776. They became the United States of America. The British government opposed this independence. It sent more troops to the colonies. The war continued.

Benjamin Franklin was an author, a scientist, and a politician.

In 1782, Benjamin Franklin wrote a fake news story. Franklin was an ambassador to France. He was against British rule. He claimed the king of England had ordered the killings of hundreds of people. He said the murderers were Native Americans who were allied with the king. This was not true. But Franklin's story quickly spread. Newspapers in some of the colonies printed it. Many people believed it.

The Revolutionary War ended in 1783. The colonists won the war. Colonists wrote the US Constitution in 1787. It outlined the nation's laws. Ten **amendments**

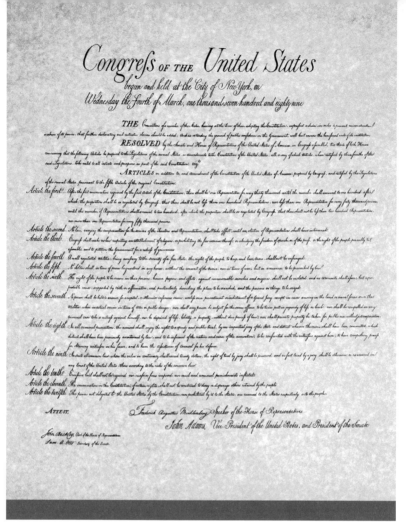

The Bill of Rights outlines important rights and freedoms guaranteed to US citizens.

were added to the constitution in 1791.

These amendments are called the Bill of

Rights. The First Amendment says that the

US Congress cannot take away a person's

right to free speech. Free speech is the

freedom to express ideas and opinions.

The amendment also promised freedom

of the press. This meant that media had

the right to share news. The government

would not **censor** or control the media. The

amendment did not say that what the press

printed had to be true.

FAKE NEWS AND POLITICS

In the 1790s, newspapers continued

to print whatever they wanted. Some

newspapers promoted political parties.

The *Gazette of the United States* published

the opinions of the Federalist Party.

The *National Gazette* reported the views of the Democratic-Republican Party. These were opposing parties. The papers attacked each other. They sometimes made claims about the other paper that were not true.

YELLOW JOURNALISM

In the 1890s, the *New York World* and *New York Journal* used shocking headlines to attract readers. In 1895, the *World* published a cartoon called *Hogan's Alley*. It featured a character dressed in yellow clothes. His name was "the yellow kid." This cartoon became popular. The *Journal* hired the cartoonist away from the *World*. This battle between the papers gave rise to the term *yellow journalism*. The term describes sensational storytelling.

James Madison and Thomas Jefferson were Democratic-Republicans. They helped start the *National Gazette*. Madison and Jefferson believed freedom of the press is key to democracy. Jefferson said that he would prefer "newspapers without a government" to "a government without newspapers."[2] The press allows people's opinions to be heard. Some people call the press a government watchdog. This is because it watches over people in power. It makes sure leaders respect people's rights and freedoms. It can point out when politicians are not telling the truth.

PRESIDENTS AND THE PRESS

In 1801, Jefferson was elected president. His opinion of the press changed. The press watched him closely. Jefferson had lived in France. He agreed with France on many issues. The nation had been founded mostly by British colonists. Many of them disagreed with Jefferson's views. Jefferson also had unpopular ideas about religion.

Some newspapers criticized Jefferson. Jefferson did not like what the press said about him. Sometimes the press's claims were true. But sometimes they were false. In 1806, Jefferson wrote that "nothing

Thomas Jefferson was president from 1801 to 1809.

can now be believed which is seen in

a newspaper."[3]

Jefferson had some newspaper editors

charged with **sedition**. Sedition is the act

People who were charged with sedition were tried in court.

of printing untrue or vicious words about

a person in power. The Sedition Act made

it a crime to print mean-spirited words

about politicians if those words were not true. Jefferson had fought against passing the Sedition Act before he was elected. This act had been passed into law in 1798. As president, Jefferson changed his mind about the Sedition Act. He used the act to his advantage. He tried to silence his critics.

Since Jefferson, many presidents have clashed with the press. These disagreements often occur during wars or other challenges. Many news outlets criticized Trump during his presidency. Trump often attacked the press. His attacks were direct. He called certain reporters dishonest. He dismissed the watchdog role of the press. He called the press an "enemy of the people."[4] He used the term fake news to discredit the press. He also used the term to dismiss stories that he did not like. For example, he dismissed the story about Russians spreading fake news.

Some people worry that attacks on the press could lead to bigger problems. William McRaven is a retired US Navy officer. He said, "The president's attack on the media is the greatest threat to our democracy."[5] McRaven believes an attack

NIXON AND THE PRESS

In 1972, President Richard Nixon was up for reelection. Nixon was a Republican. He hired men to break into the main office of the Democratic Party. The men installed listening devices. They wanted to spy on the Democrats. Police arrested the men. *Washington Post* reporters learned about Nixon's role. Nixon disliked the press. He created a list of reporters that he called his enemies. He ordered the Federal Bureau of Investigation to spy on them. Nixon was forced to resign in 1974.

on the media is an attack on free speech.

Many people agree. They worry that

some people use the term fake news to

silence others.

CHAPTER TWO

WHY DO PEOPLE BELIEVE FAKE NEWS?

Many people believe fake news is a problem. About 25 percent of Americans visited fake news sites in the month before the 2016 election. Social media helps fake news spread quickly. Studies show that people are more likely to share false stories than true stories.

People often have many different news sources to choose from.

This often makes fake news spread faster than real news.

Fake news stories appeal to people's emotions. They are full of details. People often share emotional stories before reading through them. They think the story must be

true because they agree with its views. They

tend to share the story with people who

have similar views. Others read and share

the story. Then fake news can go **viral**.

CONFIRMING BELIEFS

Websites monitor people's computer

activity. They collect data about other sites

BOTS TO BLAME?

Some people claim that bots are the reason for the spread of fake news. But studies have shown that bots tend to share the same amount of fake and real news. Bots may be part of the problem. But they are not entirely to blame. People spread a lot of fake news too.

a person visits. This can give information about a person's interests. The sites show users other content they may like. This content may be ads or news. For example, Facebook collects user data. It has 1.7 billion users. It tracks the posts that users like and share. Some posts may be fake news. Facebook feeds users content that is similar to these posts. In this way, users can be exposed to more fake news. They may only be fed news from a few sources. These sources may appear often on a user's feed. This process limits the types of stories a user sees.

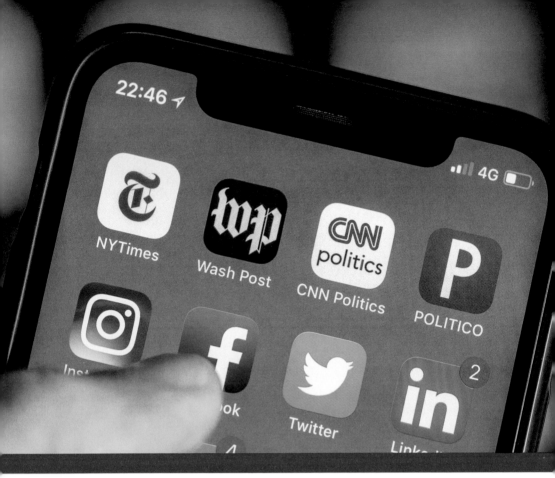

Many people get news from phone apps.

People seek out stories that match

their point of view. News feeds reinforce

their beliefs. They are not exposed to

different points of view. They often do

not think critically about stories that they

ALEX JONES

Fake news can have devastating consequences. Alex Jones runs a fake news website. The site is called InfoWars. Jones believes that a shooting in Newton, Connecticut, never happened. The shooting happened at Sandy Hook Elementary School in 2012. The shooter killed twenty-six people. Twenty of the victims were children. Jones said the parents of the victims were actors. Some people believe his stories. They harassed the families of the shooting victims. Some families received death threats.

agree with. They do not consider whether the stories may be true. Brendan Nyhan is a professor at the University of Michigan. He says, "I don't think we want [social media] deciding what kinds of news and information are shown to people."[6]

FAKE PHOTOS AND VIDEOS

Fake news is not only text. Some people create fake images or videos. Computer artists alter photographs to make them look real. They may add something to the photo, such as a person. They may move parts of the photo around. This can change the photo's meaning. Some artists create fake photos to make a point. They try to show how convincing fake photos can be. They encourage people to study images before sharing them. Some artists create fake

Artist Scott Reeder created a sculpture about fake news in 2013. It was put outside Trump International Hotel and Tower in Chicago, Illinois, in 2017.

photos as satire. Satire exaggerates the

facts. It pokes fun at people's beliefs. But

other artists want to convince people that

a fake image is real. They want to spread

fake news.

Some people create fake photos of unidentified flying objects (UFOs), or alien space ships.

Artists who create fake photos usually do not label the photos as fake. This can make it hard for people to recognize them as fake. People tend to believe what they see. Fake images and videos are more likely to go viral than text. The more shocking the image, the more likely people will share it.

VIRAL FAKE NEWS

In 2017, a photo of Trump went viral. It appeared to show Trump rescuing people during a flood in Houston, Texas. In the photo, Trump floats on a raft. He hands a "Make America Great Again" hat to a person in the floodwaters. "Make America Great Again" was Trump's slogan in the 2016 presidential campaign. But the flood shown in the photo occurred in 2015. Trump was not yet president. Someone had added him into the photo. In the photo, Trump is wearing a suit and tie. This was another clue that the photo was fake. Yet it was shared 275,000 times on Facebook. Trump supporters thought the image proved that the president had helped flood victims.

Sometimes even government officials spread fake news. In November 2018, Sarah Sanders posted a video. Sanders was the White House press secretary. The video shows an angry Trump telling a reporter to sit down. The reporter was Jim Acosta. He works for CNN. Acosta was asking questions that Trump did not want to answer. The video shows a White House intern pulling the microphone away

The Trump administration banned CNN reporter Jim Acosta from the White House in November 2018.

from Acosta. Sanders claimed that Acosta

put his hands on the intern. An expert

reviewed the video that Sanders posted.

The expert found that it was altered.

Acosta's arm movement had been sped

up. This made it appear as if Acosta had

touched the intern.

CHAPTER THREE

WHAT IS THE PUBLIC'S OPINION OF FAKE NEWS?

Many fake news outlets post stories daily. This makes it hard for people to trust what they read. Fake news has made many Americans distrust the media. In 2018, only 33 percent of Americans had a favorable opinion of the press.

Fake news sites such as InfoWars try to promote their stories as real news.

Many people agree that the media

plays an important role in a democracy.

It keeps people informed. But some think

the media is not fulfilling this role. They

think there is too much bias in the media.

Many news sources, such as Fox News, have biases.

News organizations can have bias. Many favor one political party over another. Some are critical of the government. Others support the government. Bias can affect a story's accuracy. Some writers may omit facts that go against their point of view. Many news sources have bias. More than

BIAS IN THE NEWS

It is difficult for anyone to write without some sort of bias. Opinions influence the topics people choose to write about. They also shape how people write about a topic. Many young people today are aware of bias in news. Emma Neely is nineteen years old. She said, "I don't believe there [are] any neutral news organizations. Each writer and editor has their own personal bias."

Quoted in Taylor Lorenz, "Trump Has Changed How Teens View the News," The Atlantic, August 29, 2018. www.theatlantic.com.

half of Americans say they cannot name a news source that is not biased.

Many people also have trouble identifying fake news. Stanford University studied 7,804 students in 2016. The students were a variety of ages. The youngest were in middle school. The oldest were in college.

Researchers shared tweets with the

students. Tweets are Twitter posts. The

tweets were news stories. Students had to

decide which stories were real and which

were fake. Many middle school students

struggled to identify fake news. They trusted

stories that had photos and lots of details.

These factors had more influence than the

news source. Many of the stories with lots

of details and large photos were fake.

TRUST IN THE MEDIA

Older Americans tend to trust the media

more than younger Americans. Many young

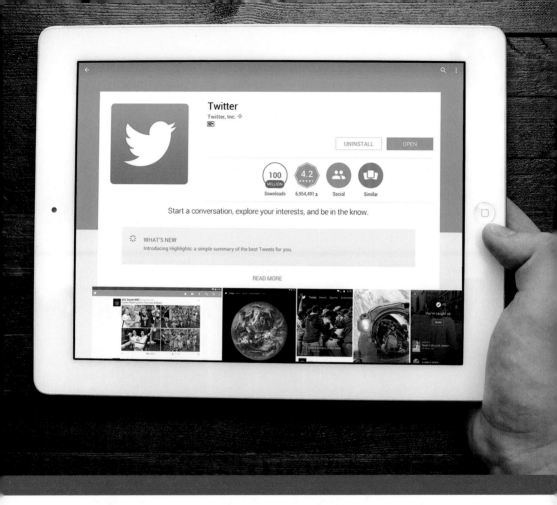

Some people use Twitter as a source of news.

Americans do not trust major news sources.

This includes CNN and the *New York*

Times. It also includes the *Washington Post*

and Fox News. Many people consider these

sources to be biased. Large companies

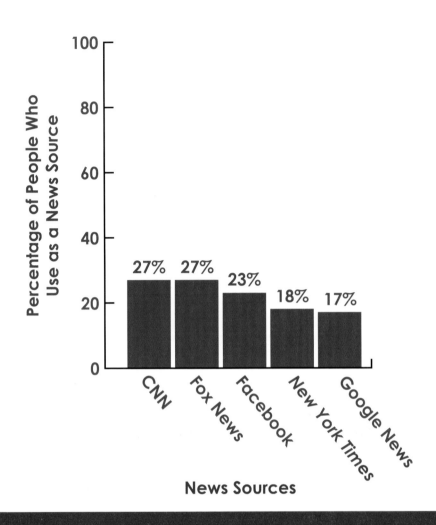

This graph shows the most popular news sources among Americans in 2017.

support these news organizations. The

companies may control what these media

outlets report.

University researchers published a study in 2019. They studied Facebook users before and after the 2016 presidential election. The study included 3,500 users. The users were a variety of ages. They allowed the researchers to look at their posts. Researchers checked the news stories users shared. They found a difference between Republicans and Democrats. Republicans were more likely to share fake news. This may have been because many fake news stories supported Trump. Researchers also found a difference between younger and older users.

Many people get their news from online sources.

Older users were those older than sixty-five.

They were more likely to share fake news.

Researchers do not know the reason for

this. But they had some ideas. Many older

users have less experience with the internet. Some also have problems with thinking and memory. These problems are common in older adults. They can affect a person's judgment.

Some people seek out news from nontraditional sources. They may follow independent journalists on social media. They may do further research if they are unsure whether a source can be trusted. They learn about the journalist's experience and background. They see if other people they trust follow the source. Then they decide if they believe the story.

SOCIAL MEDIA'S ROLE

Many people think social media helps keep the public informed. Social media is the main source of news for many young people. But fake news is widespread on these sites. Many people think social media sites need to do more to stop the spread

TWITTER AND FAKE NEWS

In 2018, *Science* magazine published a study. Researchers had studied fake news on Twitter. About 26,000 fake news stories appeared on Twitter in a ten-year period. The study found that Twitter users share fake news more often than real news. Most of this is fake political news.

of fake news. Companies could remove fake news posts on their sites. But many people do not like this idea. They do not think companies should be able to pick and choose what users can or cannot read.

CHAPTER FOUR

WHO IS FIGHTING FAKE NEWS?

Fighting fake news is not easy. Fake news floods the internet each day. It comes from many different sources. Many people are involved in the fight against fake news. Some are activists. Others are politicians. Social media companies have gotten involved too.

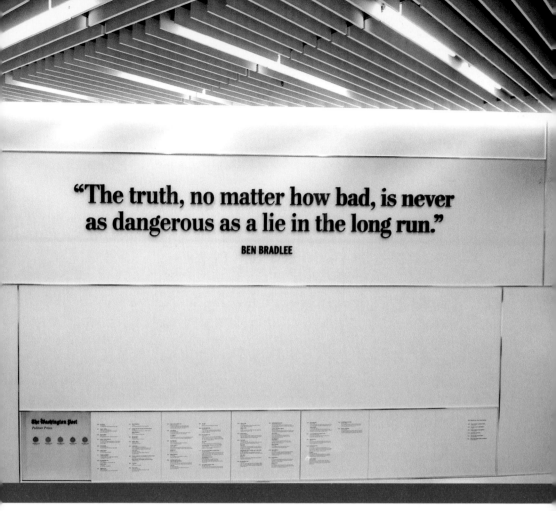

A quote about the importance of facts is on display at the Washington Post *building in Washington, DC.*

SOCIAL MEDIA

Some social media companies are trying

to stop the spread of fake news. Twitter

deleted 70 million fake accounts between

May and July 2018. YouTube gave

$25 million to news organizations.

It promised to flag false news.

Facebook hired a team of fact-checkers

in 2018. Fact-checkers examine news to

make sure it represents the facts. They

flag inaccurate content. Facebook's

fact-checkers are all around the world.

Many are journalists. They fact-check

text, photos, and videos that appear on

Facebook. Facebook promises to take

down pages that often post fake news. It is

also working to stop hate groups from using

the site. In July 2018, Facebook removed

An ad at a train stop in Chicago, Illinois, warns Facebook users about fake accounts.

a page made by a racist group. The group

was planning a rally. It never took place.

Facebook hired software engineers.

They create **algorithms**. Algorithms are

instructions that help solve problems.

The algorithms find fake Facebook accounts. Facebook also posted tips on how to spot fake news. It offers tools that help users learn more about the source

CARS

Librarians recommend using CARS to find good sources. CARS stands for credibility, accuracy, reasonableness, and support. *Credibility* means that a source can be trusted. *Accuracy* means that the source gets the facts right. People should also check a source's reasonableness. This means its reporting is believable. People should research other sources too. They can see if other sources support the news from the first source. This suggests it is a good source.

and the author. Users can learn about other stories an author has posted.

FAKE NEWS LAWS

Some countries have passed laws to limit fake news. Germany was the first to do so. Germany's law was passed in June 2017. It forces social media sites to remove fake news. Sites also must remove hate speech. This includes Holocaust denial. The Holocaust occurred in the 1930s and 1940s. The Nazi Party ruled Germany. Nazis targeted Jewish people. They killed Jewish people and many others. Some researchers estimate they killed 15 million

German chancellor Angela Merkel helped pass Germany's fake news law in 2017.

to 20 million people. Some people deny the Holocaust happened. Holocaust denial is illegal in Germany. It is not considered free speech. It is punishable by up to five years in prison.

Germany's law says sites must take down illegal content within twenty-four hours. The site must pay a fine if the content is not removed. The law went into effect on January 1, 2018. It was passed in response to racist content that spread on social media. Facebook hired hundreds of staff members in Germany to help enforce the law.

In April 2018, Malaysia passed the Anti-Fake News Act. The act was passed before elections. Fears quickly surfaced. People claimed the law prevented free speech. Human rights activists were concerned. Many thought the government was trying to silence people who were against those in power. The law did not clearly define fake news. The government could claim that any news it disagrees with is fake. The law required people who publish fake news to remove it. The punishment for breaking this law was a large fine and a prison sentence. The sentence was up to six years in prison. Many people opposed the law. As a result, the government overturned it. This happened in August 2018. Malaysia was the first country to overturn a fake news law.

Emmanuel Macron was elected president of France in 2017.

In France, President Emmanuel Macron helped pass a fake news law in November 2018. The law allows judges to remove fake news from websites during elections. Macron worried that other countries would try to sway elections. He pointed to Russia's interference in the 2016 US presidential election. Some people in France dislike this law. They think it suppresses their right to free speech.

LAWS IN THE UNITED STATES

No federal laws limit fake news in the United States. But in 2017, US senators proposed a bill. The bill is called the Honest Ads Act. It would require some companies to keep copies of political ads. The companies would include Facebook and Google. They would have to share information about the ad buyer. They would also have to

Librarians and teachers educate students about how to find reliable sources.

share data on anyone who spends more

than $500 on these ads each year. This

could expose people who try to influence

elections. The act is still being considered.

Some states have passed **media literacy** laws. Media literacy involves studying news sources. It teaches people how to tell if a source is trustworthy. California passed a law in 2018. It encourages the teaching of media literacy in schools. It requires the California Department of Education site to list media literacy resources. Other states have passed similar laws.

TAKING RESPONSIBILITY

Internet users can also fight fake news. Users should read posts all the way through before sharing them. One study found

TEACHING MEDIA LITERACY

Media literacy classes teach students how to spot good sources. Students learn how to use fact-checking sites. These sites include Snopes, FactCheck.org, and PolitiFact. They explain whether popular news stories are accurate. Students also research the group that posted the story. Political groups may not be trustworthy. Students learn how to do an internet search. They look through the results to find the most reliable source.

that six out of ten links were forwarded without the user reading the article. Experts recommend that users think before sharing a post. Users might wait before sharing a post that stirs up outrage. Posts that play on people's emotions may be fake news.

A protester pokes fun at Trump's definition of fake news at a march in 2018.

Users can first do research. They can read other articles on the topic. The articles should come from reliable sources. They should also come from a variety of sources. Users should read articles that offer different points of view. This allows users to get a well-rounded view of the topic.

The spread of fake news could be reduced if people follow these guidelines. Michael Socolow is a journalism professor. He says, "We should be thinking about what [it means] to trust our sources of information. It's now on us . . . to be much more skeptical."[7]

GLOSSARY

algorithms

instructions that help a computer solve a problem

allied

partnered with someone or something

amendments

changes or additions to an existing law

bias

an author's opinion or point of view that shapes the way an article or post is written

censor

to make media content unavailable to the public

colonies

settlements on land owned by a faraway country or nation

conspiracy theories

beliefs that powerful organizations are secretly causing certain events

media literacy

the ability to study and evaluate media

viral

something that spreads quickly and becomes popular

SOURCE NOTES

INTRODUCTION: THE SPREAD OF FAKE NEWS

1. Quoted in Mike Wendling, "The (Almost) Complete History of 'Fake News,'" *BBC*, January 22, 2018. www.bbc.com.

CHAPTER ONE: WHAT IS FAKE NEWS?

2. Quoted in Lindsey Bever, "Memo to Donald Trump: Thomas Jefferson Invented Hating the Media," *Washington Post*, February 18, 2017. www.washingtonpost.com.

3. Quoted in Lindsey Bever, "Memo to Donald Trump: Thomas Jefferson Invented Hating the Media."

4. Quoted in Emily Stewart, "Trump Calls the Media the 'True Enemy of the People' the Same Day a Bomb Is Sent to CNN," *Vox*, October 29, 2018. www.vox.com.

5. Quoted in Andrew Kragie, "Everything's Political to Trump, Even Killing Osama Bin Laden," *Atlantic*, November 19, 2018. www.theatlantic.com.

CHAPTER TWO: WHY DO PEOPLE BELIEVE FAKE NEWS?

6. Quoted in Robinson Meyer, "Why It's Okay to Call It 'Fake News,'" *Atlantic*, March 9, 2018. www.theatlantic.com.

CHAPTER FOUR: WHO IS FIGHTING FAKE NEWS?

7. Quoted in Carl Holm, "The Radio Drama That Shocked America 80 Years Ago and the Modern Birth of Fake News," *Deutsche Welle*, October 26, 2018. www.dw.com.

FOR FURTHER RESEARCH

BOOKS

Duchess Harris, JD, PhD, *The Fake News Phenomenon*. Minneapolis, MN: Abdo Publishing, 2018.

Wil Mara, *Fake News*. North Mankato, MN: Cherry Lake Publishing, 2019.

INTERNET SOURCES

Beth Hewitt, "How to Spot Fake News—An Expert's Guide for Young People," *The Conversation*, December 8, 2017. www.theconversation.com.

"How to Identify Fake News in 10 Steps," *ProQuest*, n.d. www.proquest.com/blog.

"Spotting Fake News," *National Geographic*, n.d. www.kids.nationalgeographic.com.

WEBSITES

AllSides
www.allsides.com

This website gives three sides to each news topic to help readers understand the news from different points of view.

FactCheck.org
www.factcheck.org

This fact-checking website gives people information on which news stories are real and which are fake.

PolitiFact
www.politifact.com

This website fact-checks news stories. It provides the true story behind topics currently in the news. It also shares reliable sources so readers can do further research.

INDEX

IMAGE CREDITS

ABOUT THE AUTHOR

Kari Cornell is a writer and editor who likes to cook, craft, and tinker in the garden. She has written many books for young readers, including *The Nitty Gritty Gardening Book, Dig In: 12 Easy Gardening Projects Using Kitchen Scraps*, and *The Craft-a-Day Book*.